T0071036

AMY BEACH

arr. Robert Gower

SCOTTISH LEGEND

MUSIC DEPARTMENT

OXFORD
UNIVERSITY PRESS

Scottish Legend

from *Two Piano Pieces*, Op. 54

AMY BEACH
(1867–1944)
arr. Robert Gower

© Oxford University Press 2019

Printed in Great Britain

OXFORD UNIVERSITY PRESS, MUSIC DEPARTMENT, GREAT CLARENDON STREET, OXFORD OX2 6DP

The Moral Rights of the Composer have been asserted. Photocopying this copyright material is ILLEGAL.

10
pp
13
ritenuto
16
lunga
pp
mf
poco più animato
cresc.
20
f
dim.

24
rit.
a tempo
3
pp
cresc.
ff
sostenuto
28
rit.
lunga
3
pp
dolcissimo
31
rall.
lunga
pp
più tranquillo
34
molto ritenuto
lunga
ppp